30 SECOND
MYSTERIES
VOLUME II

Warning: Small parts may be a choking hazard. Not for children under 3 years.

Editorial Director: Erin Conley
Designer: Lucy Nielsen and Jeanette Miller
Special thanks to Amanda Banks, Christine Brenneman, Suzanne Cracraft,
Connie Gee, Gary Hornbeek, Sara Huong, Emily Jocson, Moss Kardner, Susan King,
Jeff Pinsker, Tami Sartor, Rosie Slattery, Lani Stackel and Jim Stern for their
invaluable assistance and contributions!

ISBN 1-57528-915-6

04 MC 9 8 7 6 5 4 3 2

CONTENTS

INTRODUCTION 4

RULES 5

WHO 7

WHAT 65

WHERE 123

WHY 181

Ready for a mystery? How did two worn-out board game inventors come up with a quiz format that has lasted a decade and entertained people as a board game, calendar and book series? I say series because this book is Volume II of 30 Second Mysteries™, the concept that Jeff Pinsker and I developed back in 1994.

Each 30 Second Mystery is a fun, interactive form of a good old-fashioned whodunit. This new collection of cases promises to entertain you, your friends and your colleagues for hours, and is sure to exercise your logical and critical-thinking muscles, no matter how strong (or flabby) they are. I had a great time putting these mysteries together and hope that you have even more fun trying to solve them.

We are already working on Volume III and would love your help. Write your own 30 Second Mystery with five clues and submit it to me through my publisher, University Games. If we include it in the next edition, we will list your name as a contributor in the credits and you can truly be part of the story. By the way, to solve the mystery of how we came up with the 30 Second Mysteries concept, check out the introduction in the original book (Volume I).

Good luck!

Bob Moog

RULES

OBJECT

To be the first player or team to solve 7 mysteries or score 7 points.

PLAYING THE GAME

• First things first: grab a pen and paper to keep track of your points.

• The youngest player spins first to determine the type of mystery to be solved (i.e. Who, What, Where, or Why) and reads the first Case and Mystery from that category out loud to the group. This player acts solely as a reader and may not play until the mystery is solved. The player to the left of the Reader gets the first clue—and the first stab at solving the mystery.

• *If a player guesses the mystery incorrectly (or doesn't have a guess)*, the player to his/her left gets the next clue and may then try to crack the case. Play proceeds in a clockwise fashion.

• *If a player guesses the mystery correctly,* s/he earns a point and the player to the Reader's left becomes the new Reader for the next case in the same category. Do not spin again until each player has read a mystery to the group.

• Once all players have acted as the Reader, it is time to spin again! The player to the left of the last person to spin now spins to determine the type of mystery to be solved. S/he is the first reader for this round.

• *Tip:* Don't forget to jot down the number of the last mystery solved in case you spin the same category more than once, which is likely to happen.

SCORING

First player to guess the mystery scores 1 point. If a player solves the mystery without hearing any clues, s/he earns 2 points.

WINNING THE GAME

The first player to score 7 points wins!

PLAYING ON YOUR OWN

Spin and read the Case and Mystery topic question from the appropriate category. Try to solve the Case using as few clues as possible.

SCORING:

10 points = 0 clues revealed
 6 points = 1 clue revealed
 5 points = 2 clues revealed
 4 points = 3 clues revealed
 3 points = 4 clues revealed
 2 points = 5 clues revealed
 0 points = Incorrect guess!

Read 10 mysteries. Collect 40 points or more and you're a winner!

WHO

30 SECOND
MYSTERIES

WHO

Case 1

THE CASE

A man stretches as far as he can to save a woman from falling fifty feet below, but misses. Without a scratch on her body, the woman stands up and walks away smiling.

THE MYSTERY

Who is the woman and why does she survive the fall unscathed?

THE CLUES

A crowd watches the accident nervously but does nothing to help.
Even though the man fails to catch her, she does not hold a grudge.
The woman's life is never truly in any danger.
The woman works hard for a living, but is a real swinger.
The woman performs under a big tent.

CASE 1 SOLUTION

The woman is a trapeze artist who misses her catch. She survives the fall because she lands in the safety net.

30 SECOND
MYSTERIES

Case 2

THE CASE

A boy enters the bedroom of a young woman and her siblings. He does not use the door to enter, even though the young woman's room is three floors up. His primary purpose is to find something he's left behind. When his business is concluded, he leaves by the same means he used to arrive.

THE MYSTERY

Who is the boy and what was he looking for?

THE CLUES

The boy is famous for his adventures.

The young woman is British.

The young woman and her siblings are little Darlings.

The boy felt as though he'd lost part of himself.

Some say the boy will never grow up.

The boy is Peter Pan.
He was looking for his shadow.

THE CASE

Stevie weighed about 100 pounds and stood about 5 feet tall. He didn't speak English and could not see. He wasn't able to walk but he could run. He was spotted last January in Ely, Minnesota, but disappeared a few days later, never to be seen again.

THE MYSTERY

Who is Stevie and why did he disappear?

THE CLUES

Stevie often made people smile.

Stevie smoked a pipe and never said a word.

Stevie was pleasingly plump.

Stevie perished in the snow.

Stevie wasn't reserved, but some people thought he had a frosty side.

CASE 3 SOLUTION

Stevie is a snowman and he melted.

THE CASE

Bill finds himself in a very dark place surrounded by a variety of precious metals. He has had a very busy day. He spends time in a taxi, visits a newsstand, stops by a corner deli and goes to the movies. He doesn't know where he will go tomorrow, but he will probably go alone. One is, after all, Bill's favorite number.

THE MYSTERY

Who is Bill and where is he?

THE CLUES

People can never seem to get enough of Bill.

Bill is not a living person.

Bill sometimes gets quartered, but he never dies.

Bill is currently in a locked box surrounded by money.

Bill's favorite president is George Washington.

Bill is a $1 bill of U.S. currency and he is in a cash register.

30 SECOND MYSTERIES

WHO

- - - - - - - - - - - - - - -

Case 5

THE CASE

A man walks into a home with a snake and goes to the bathroom. The owner frets and hovers while the man wrestles with the snake behind closed doors. The man exits the house a half hour later fatigued and sweaty, but victorious. The owner breathes a sigh of relief and gives the man a large sum of money for his efforts.

THE MYSTERY

Who is the man and what has he done?

THE CLUES

The man works hard for a living.

The man sometimes discovers small valuable goods while he works.

The man helps clear things up for people.

The man uses the snake as a tool.

The man likes a good pipe, but he doesn't smoke.

- -

CASE 5 SOLUTION

He is a plumber who has just unclogged a drain.

Case 6

THE CASE

Deep in the woods, a portly and unassuming fellow ambles along humming to himself. He finds a large hole in the ground, which he figures must house some animal, maybe a rabbit. He squirms into the hole, but on the way back out manages to get quite stuck because of his formidable girth. Finally, a little boy comes along and rescues him by pulling him out.

THE MYSTERY

Who is this individual and where does he live?

CLUES

He's from Great Britain.

When he wears clothes at all, he usually just sports a t-shirt.

He feels most at home in the woods.

His favorite food is honey.

A diminutive pig is his best friend.

Winnie the Pooh lives in the Hundred Acre Wood.

THE CASE

A stranger barges into a house where two small children wait alone for their mother to come home. The children are scared, but the stranger doesn't seem to notice. Instead, this individual makes the children play games they don't want to play. Eventually the stranger leaves but, surprisingly, the police are not summoned.

THE MYSTERY

Who is the individual and who made him famous?

THE CLUES

The individual arrives wearing a hat, gloves, a bow tie and a fur coat.
The individual brings two Things to the house.
The individual likes to play, even on a cold, cold, wet day.
A famous Dr. brought him to life.
The individual speaks in rhyme.

CASE 7 SOLUTION

The individual is the Cat in the Hat.
Dr. Seuss (Theodor Geisel) made him famous.

30 SECOND MYSTERIES

Case 8

THE CASE

A car pulls up the driveway of Mr. & Mrs. Stone. A stranger gets out of the car and rings the doorbell. Mrs. Stone peeks through the curtains and yells for her teenage daughter Vickie to stay upstairs. Mr. Stone opens the door and he and the stranger talk in hushed voices. The stranger is let inside and asks for Vickie. As Mr. Stone goes to get the girl, Mrs. Stone starts to cry.

THE MYSTERY

Who is the stranger and where does he plan to take Vickie?

THE CLUES

Mr. Stone told the stranger to take care of Vickie.

Mrs. Stone cautions Vickie to be careful.

Mr. and Mrs. Stone can't believe this is happening.

It is May and Vickie is a senior in high school.

Mr. & Mrs. Stone take a picture for posterity's sake and tell Vickie they'll see her at midnight.

The stranger is Vickie's date. He is taking her to the prom.

THE CASE

A man leaves his rowdy travel companions to seek some peace and quiet. After a long walk, he hears a voice telling him to return to his group. He returns feeling better, and carries with him some important instructions he discovered at the end of his walk. To his surprise, the rowdy group is entirely out of control and has surrounded a large farm animal.

THE MYSTERY

Who is the man and where is he?

THE CLUES

The man and his group are near a famous mountain.

The man's long walk lasted several days.

The group of people numbered in the thousands.

The farm animal was made of gold.

The country was Egypt.

CASE 9 SOLUTION

The man is Moses and the place is Mount Sinai.

THE CASE

A man finds himself surrounded by hostile strangers who literally want a piece of him. He flees, but encounters fierce animals and natural obstacles. Finally, he places his trust in a friendly stranger, only to be betrayed and murdered.

THE MYSTERY

Who is the man and who betrays him?

THE CLUES

The man is fond of speaking in rhymes.

He can't swim, but the friendly stranger can.

Before his escape, the man is kept in an oven.

The friendly stranger is known for his clever and foxy demeanor.

The man is irresistibly sweet.

*The man is the Gingerbread Man
who was eaten by a fox.*

THE CASE

A patriot travels on a small horse to a faraway village. Upon arriving, he places part of a nearby bird into his clothing. He then appears quite confused by pronouncing to all within earshot that he has in his possession some Italian pasta.

THE MYSTERY

Who is the patriot and what is the Italian pasta?

CLUES

He is visiting a city on the East Coast.

Most people learn about him even before they enter school.

He was popular during the forming of our nation.

His name identifies him as a "Northerner."

His story is continually repeated in song.

*The patriot is Yankee Doodle Dandy
and the pasta is macaroni.*

30 SECOND
MYSTERIES

WHO

Case 12

THE CASE

A woman is a contract killer. Strangely enough, the police are not interested in arresting her. She is always invited into the very homes where her murders are scheduled to take place. Her work is conducted in front of witnesses and no one even tries to stop her from killing.

THE MYSTERY

Who is this woman and how does she kill her victims?

THE CLUES

The woman never uses a gun to kill.

Anyone can identify her by her work dress.

After a year on the job, she's likely killed thousands, maybe even millions.

She usually has to wear a mask when she is working.

She often makes repeat visits to the same house.

The woman is a professional exterminator.
She poisons her victims.

30 SECOND MYSTERIES

WHO

Case 13

THE CASE

One man's image has inspired many people to write songs, stories and poems. He has even compelled some to travel great distances to visit him. For as long as anyone can remember, individuals around the world have seen him on a regular basis. However, he only shows his face from a distance; when people are able to reach him, he disappears.

THE MYSTERY

Who is this man and which of his features are people able to see?

THE CLUES

He is surrounded by stars, but he's not an actor.
Ancient Greeks believed he was a woman.
Farmers, fishermen and hunters look to him for advice.
He appears ageless and timeless.
He shows himself when it gets dark out.

CASE 13 SOLUTION

He is the Man in the Moon, whose face people see when gazing into space.

THE CASE

A talented entertainer gathers several of his friends and his glamorous girlfriend together to make a major motion picture. In it, he performs a new song about a colorful object in the sky, which becomes an instant national hit. The star is more famous than ever before, but never receives a penny of the millions in proceeds.

THE MYSTERY

Who is the star and who is his girlfriend?

THE CLUES

The year is 1979.
The song is considered dreamy.
The star hosted a weekly TV show with celebrity guests.
The star's girlfriend wears a blonde wig.
The star's favorite color is green.

*The star is Kermit the Frog
and his girlfriend is Miss Piggy.*

THE CASE

As Vera idly watches, a well-dressed man speaks to her fluently and rapidly about pressing social issues. Eventually, Vera tires of his conversation. With a slight movement of her hand, she dismisses him and he vanishes into thin air.

THE MYSTERY

Who is the man and what did Vera do to dismiss him?

THE CLUES

Vera has no magical powers.

Vera can speak to the man, but he can't hear her.

The man is seated but Vera can't see his legs.

Every day the man informs people about important events.

Vera sits in her living room, but the man never comes to her home.

The man is a TV news reporter;
Vera turned off the TV with the remote control.

Case 16

THE CASE

While taking a midnight stroll, Marvin is viciously attacked. After he quickly rubs something all over his body, the attackers flee. His assailants don't have weapons, but Marvin has definitely lost some blood.

THE MYSTERY

Who is attacking Marvin and what substance drives them away?

THE CLUES

At night it is almost impossible to see the attackers.
Marvin killed a few of them with his bare hands.
Though Marvin can't press charges, he's itching for revenge.
He bought the protective substance at a drug store.
His attackers didn't kick or punch, but they did a lot of biting.

Marvin is bitten by mosquitoes that stay away after he applies insect repellant.

Case 17

THE CASE

A woman sits in a dark room furiously washing her hands. She appears terribly upset and has a crazed look in her eye. There is a man and another woman in the room with her, and they listen to the woman's almost unintelligible ramblings with horror.

THE MYSTERY

Who is this woman and what is she trying to wash off her hands?

THE CLUES

The woman is a Lady, but not a tramp.

The woman is upset because she is overcome by guilt about something she and her husband have done.

Her hands are not dirty.

She will eventually die by her own hand.

The woman and her husband are characters in a famous tragedy about greed and ambition.

CASE 17 SOLUTION

The woman is Shakespeare's Lady Macbeth. She is trying to wash (imagined) blood from her hands.

30 SECOND MYSTERIES

WHO

Case 18

THE CASE

A little girl finds fame, fortune and privilege. The girl's hairstyle and endorsement of a famous ship make national news, but she also achieves important accomplishments decades later in the field of international affairs.

THE MYSTERY

Who is this very famous little girl and what famous ship did she endorse?

THE CLUES

The little girl has been a colonel, a rebel, a princess and more.

For years, women copied her hairstyle.

She is known for her singing and tap dancing.

She turned Black when she got married.

In her second career, her dimples helped advance diplomacy.

She is Shirley Temple (Black).
She endorsed the "Good Ship Lollipop."

Case 19

THE CASE

The stars of a TV show are upset that they were chosen. They will probably not be on the next episode or, if they are, it will be their last appearance. They do not audition; they are chosen by the producers and by America.

THE MYSTERY

Who are the stars and on what show are they featured?

THE CLUES

The audience doesn't vote but the producers hope they'll call in.

The stars' actions are often reenacted.

The show is nonfiction.

The show helps a government agency do important work.

The host of the show continually asks America for its help.

The stars are criminals wanted by the police and the FBI. They are featured on America's Most Wanted.

30 SECOND MYSTERIES

WHO

Case 20

THE CASE

Parker crouches under a table in his house, fearing for his life. His two brothers have already been attacked and he knows he may be next when the enemy finds him. Moments later, he hears his enemy taunting him but he remains in seclusion, hoping for the best. After surviving a huge blast, Parker knows he is finally safe for good.

THE MYSTERY

Who is Parker and who is his enemy?

THE CLUES

Parker is smarter than his brothers.
Parker's enemy is large, intimidating and very hairy.
Parker's enemy has strong lungs.
Parker's house is made of brick.
Parker's enemy enjoys a good pork chop.

Parker is one of the Three Little Pigs.
The Big Bad Wolf is his enemy.

THE CASE

One fateful day in a courthouse in the American South, a young litigator hears the disturbing tale of a girl's rape. He is so moved by the story that he changes the direction of his life permanently. From that point on, he wakes up early to pursue this new passion that will one day make him quite wealthy.

THE MYSTERY

Who is the man and what does he become?

THE CLUES

The man was a member of the Mississippi House of Representatives for seven years.

An attorney by training, the man now makes his living at a computer.

The man is one of modern publishing's great success stories.

Nearly all of the man's books have made it to the silver screen.

The man knows Tom Cruise, Julia Roberts and Susan Sarandon.

CASE 21 SOLUTION

---

*He is John Grisham; he became
a best-selling author.*

WHO

Case 22

THE CASE

A man builds a castle but never lives in it, despite its popularity. Even after his death, millions pay homage every year, encountering enormous beasts and witnessing terrible explosions. Though exhausted and drained of valuable resources, many feel compelled to make another pilgrimage to the castle's grounds in the future.

THE MYSTERY

Who built the castle and where is it?

THE CLUES

A TV and movie producer designed the castle.

The castle is part of a magical place.

The castle is in California.

The castle is surrounded by an amusement park.

The castle's creator brought Pinocchio to life.

CASE 22 SOLUTION

Walt Disney built the castle as part of Disneyland.

30 SECOND MYSTERIES

WHO

- - - - - - - -

Case 23

THE CASE

Anthony's wife has not been speaking to him lately. Anthony comes home early from work and sees an unfamiliar car in the driveway. He anxiously opens the door and finds his wife with another man. Anthony is startled, but says nothing and fixes himself a snack.

THE MYSTERY

Who is the man and why hasn't Anthony's wife been speaking to him?

THE CLUES

The man in the house is not a stranger.

The man in the house is carrying the tools of his trade.

Anthony's wife has been sick for several days.

Anthony's wife is fully clothed.

Anthony is hoping the man will get his wife to talk to him again.

- -

CASE 23 SOLUTION

*The man is the family doctor, who is making
a house call. Anthony's wife hasn't been speaking to
him because she has laryngitis.*

30 SECOND
MYSTERIES

THE CASE
Laurel lives a peaceful life in a wooded region of the United States. One day, a person approaches and savagely attacks Laurel with a sharp weapon. Laurel is mortally wounded and dies. The person sells Laurel's body for a good price.

THE MYSTERY
Who was Laurel and why did the person sell Laurel's body?

THE CLUES
Laurel was tall and slender.
Laurel had a quiet disposition and a sweet smell.
Although Laurel was cut with an axe, there was no blood.
Laurel's body was cut into pieces before it was sold.
Laurel is not a person.

CASE 24 SOLUTION

Laurel was a bay laurel tree.
The person sold the tree for firewood.

WHO

Case 25

THE CASE

Every day of his life a fellow confronts danger, often finding himself facing the barrel of a gun. With keen acuity, he's able to escape every time, sometimes by dodging bullets or romancing his foe, and always by poking fun at others.

THE MYSTERY

Who is this rascal and what is his favorite catchphrase?

THE CLUES

Though not a physician, he often refers to his adversary as one.

He lives underground.

Kids have enjoyed him for generations.

He hangs around with some real loonies.

His favorite food is carrots.

It's Bugs Bunny.
His favorite catchphrase is, "What's up, Doc?"

Case 26

THE CASE

Parents willingly take their children to visit an eccentric middle-aged man in his extravagant residence. They do not know the man and are very anxious about entering his home. Once inside, they must save their children from near disaster as a result of their affiliations with this man. Still, he is never charged with a single crime.

THE MYSTERY

Who is the man and where does he live?

THE CLUES

The man likes his sweets.

The children are all contest winners.

The man offers the parents and their kids a sweet deal.

Roald Dahl wrote a book about the man.

The man is also known as the Candy Man.

CASE 26 SOLUTION

The man is Willy Wonka.
He lives in a chocolate factory.

THE CASE

In the middle of the afternoon, a woman finds a hidden key and unlocks the door to a house she's never seen. She takes notes and photos of everything she sees yet takes nothing, leaving the house as quietly as she entered.

THE MYSTERY

Who is the woman and why has she entered the house?

THE CLUES

The woman is not a friend or relation of the owners.
The owners of the house were expecting the woman, but had hidden the key.
The woman has a contract with the homeowner.
The woman knows how valuable the house is.
The woman makes homes her business.

CASE 27 SOLUTION

The woman is a real estate agent and has entered the house to preview it.

30 SECOND
MYSTERIES

WHO

- - - - - - - - - - - - -

Case 28

THE CASE

Diana is not a native American, but she has served in the U.S. military. She hates crime and is an outspoken advocate for women's rights and peace. Diana is an incredible athlete, but is best known for her all-American uniform. She is an expert with a rope but has never performed in a rodeo.

THE MYSTERY

Who is this woman and where is she from originally?

THE CLUES

The woman is from the Caribbean.

The woman fights crime in her community and has been on TV.

The woman possesses super-human strength.

The woman was introduced in comic books.

Diana Prince is the woman's birth name.

CASE 28 SOLUTION

The woman is Wonder Woman.
She is from Paradise Island.

30 SECOND
MYSTERIES

WHAT

Case 1

THE CASE

Two men in white suits have worked in a large, dark room for over thirty years. They create small controlled explosions and experiment with animals. Though people have noticed some of the animals disappear, the men in white claim this is all done in the name of conservation.

THE MYSTERY

What are the men's names and what do they do for a living?

THE CLUES

They are not scientists.

They work with dangerous animals, which they also keep as pets.

They live and work in Las Vegas, but are originally from Germany.

The animals they work with also wear white.

The two men draw large paying crowds.

They are Siegfried and Roy, magicians in Las Vegas who work towards the conservation of white tigers.

WHAT

Case 2

THE CASE

Furious with her black cat, Angela attempts to shoot it. Instead, she hits and kills her elderly father, while the cat flees. To hide her crime, Angela drags her father's body into the cellar and walls up the corpse. Alerted by worried neighbors, the police investigate the cellar and, by listening carefully, quickly discover the body, along with something else quite unexpected.

THE MYSTERY

What did the police hear and what else did they find?

THE CLUES

Being dead, Angela's father was unable to make any sound.
Angela's father was not wearing anything that could make noise.
Angela was unable to see clearly in the cellar while walling up her father's body.
A similar situation took place in one of Edgar Allan Poe's stories.
Angela was shocked by what the police found.

They heard a cat meowing and found it walled in with the body of Angela's father.

30 SECOND MYSTERIES

WHAT

Case 3

THE CASE

Stan walks into a large room wearing his robe. When people see him they stop talking and look up. After a while, Stan walks away and doesn't reappear for around a week. The people all leave quietly. Some leave Stan money.

THE MYSTERY

What is Stan's profession and where does he work?

THE CLUES

Stan is not homeless or crazy.

People look up to Stan.

Stan likes to serve, but he doesn't play tennis.

Stan always works on Sunday.

Stan's not a family man, but he is a man for families.

Stan is a priest. He works in a church.

30 SECOND MYSTERIES

WHAT

Case 4

THE CASE

The deadliest animal in the United States roams the streets of a small suburban community. Every year, these animals kill more humans, in various gruesome ways, than any other species. Nonetheless, few humans are frightened of these animals; instead, they admire and even feed them.

THE MYSTERY

What are these animals called and how do they kill humans?

THE CLUES

The animals do not have large claws or fangs.

The animals don't drive cars, but they like the wide-open road.

The animals rarely attack humans.

Many people think these animals are cute.

Some people hunt these animals.

The animals are deer, which cause car accidents that kill approximately 100 people each year.

30 SECOND
MYSTERIES

WHAT

Case 5

THE CASE

A widow gives birth to a son with a slight deformity. Many in her community cruelly taunt and torment the son. When the widow tries to defend him, she is imprisoned. However, as the son grows older, he discovers his deformity has given him an unusual ability that leads to fame and fortune.

THE MYSTERY

What is the son's deformity and what special ability does he have?

THE CLUES

The widow is an entertainer and performer.
The son does not discover his unusual ability until he gets drunk.
A magic feather gives the son confidence in himself.
The widow's husband was named Jumbo.
Mother and son are both Disney characters.

CASE 5 SOLUTION

The son is Dumbo, an elephant born with enormous ears. The ears give him the ability to fly.

30 SECOND
MYSTERIES

WHAT

Case 6

THE CASE

The young son of a single mother leaves his home to trespass on his neighbor's property. While there, he steals from the neighbor and takes off all his clothes before running back home. Although he is seen and chased, he is not caught and no charges are pressed.

THE MYSTERY

What is the son's name and whose property does he steal?

THE CLUES

The thief has three sisters.

His father was killed by the same neighbor.

He wears only a blue jacket and clogs.

He is a famous literary character.

He has distinctive ears.

The son is Peter Rabbit and he steals
Mr. McGregor's vegetables.

30 SECOND MYSTERIES

WHAT

Case 7

THE CASE

Maria takes small, painstaking steps every night, often using a stick to help her along. Strangers watch her, but no one ever offers to help. The threat of Maria stumbling causes some people to shield their eyes.

THE MYSTERY

What is Maria's livelihood and where can she be found?

THE CLUES

Maria isn't sick or old.

Flashy outfits make up most of her wardrobe.

Her job requires a fine-tuned physique.

She really looks down on her audience.

Her whole family is in on the act.

Maria is a tightrope walker at the circus.

Case 8

THE CASE

Dr. Griffith is a successful surgeon. One day, a car hits his son, badly injuring him. Dr. Griffith rushes him to the emergency room, but upon seeing the attending surgeon, Dr. Griffith realizes it's impossible for the surgeon to operate on his son.

THE MYSTERY

What is the name of the attending surgeon and why couldn't the surgeon operate?

THE CLUES

Dr. Griffith knows the attending surgeon well.

The attending surgeon is very skilled.

The attending surgeon had not been drinking and was in no way incapacitated.

No one would expect the surgeon to operate under these conditions.

The attending surgeon knows Dr. Griffith's son intimately.

The attending surgeon is Dr. Griffith's wife, also called Dr. Griffith, who can't operate on her own child.

30 SECOND MYSTERIES

WHAT

Case 9

THE CASE

A man puts on makeup and a strange outfit as he prepares for work. What he does for a living makes some people laugh, but his main audience just wants to kill him. Though he always wears loud obnoxious clothes, he really only wants one individual's attention.

THE MYSTERY

What does the man do for a living and whose attention does he want?

THE CLUES

He has an elaborate performance but he's not an actor.

He works in a ring, but it's not one of three.

He works with animals, but they're not trained to do tricks.

He doesn't work in Hollywood, but he still deals with a lot of bull.

He looks like a joker, but his job is very serious.

The man works as a rodeo clown who tries to distract the bull from the fallen rider.

30 SECOND
MYSTERIES

WHAT

Case 10

THE CASE

Each working day, Celeste seems to run in circles to get things done. Instead of becoming frustrated by the repetitive nature of her daily responsibilities, she thrives on them. As she sees it, speed is her friend—and the faster she gets through her paces, the better.

THE MYSTERY

What is Celeste's job and why doesn't she mind it?

THE CLUES

She often gets into scrapes with her co-workers.
To be effective, she sometimes has to put her foot down.
If things get out of control, blood will spill.
Timing is everything in this line of work.
Her professional attire includes a helmet.

*She's a professional racecar driver
who loves circling the track.*

THE CASE

An entire town watches a man in a bright uniform save hundreds of lives every day. The hero has a special sign that gives him this life-saving power, but it is not a ring or a symbol on his chest. He is an elderly man with white hair and a slow step, yet he can stop a fast-moving truck with one hand.

THE MYSTERY

What do people call this man and from what kind of symbol does he draw his power?

THE CLUES

He can stop all kinds of vehicles, but he's no good against a speeding bullet.
Most kids know him well, but he's not in the movies or comic books.
He protects all types of people, but most often he's required to help children.
His sign is red and white.
He is most useful during rush hour.

*The man is a crossing guard
who uses a stop sign to control traffic.*

30 SECOND MYSTERIES

WHAT

Case 12

THE CASE

A man secretly goes to see a woman who he's known for many months. Together, they talk intimately and at one point, he even breaks down and cries. After a while, the woman writes something down on a piece of paper, gives it to him, and tells him he has to leave. With hunched shoulders, he goes out, planning to return as soon as she'll let him.

THE MYSTERY

What is the woman's relationship to the man and what did she write down during their visit?

THE CLUES

She has similar experiences many times each week.

The man stares at the ceiling much of the time they're together.

The woman is a good listener.

The woman is well educated and displays a framed diploma to prove it.

The man expects the woman to help him help himself.

The woman is the man's psychiatrist; she wrote him a prescription for anti-depressants.

Case 13

THE CASE

Nick buys a small package from an unknown man. The package's contents are colorful but explosive, and must be protected by a specialized metal lining. Nick tucks the package underneath his coat and delivers it to a young girl. Upon opening it, the little girl is not alarmed—in fact, she is delighted by what she finds.

THE MYSTERY

What does the package contain and why isn't the girl harmed?

THE CLUES

The product is not illegal in the U.S.
The package can easily fit in the man's pocket.
The package is lined with aluminum foil.
The little girl immediately put the contents in her mouth.
Legend has it that combining the product with Coke® is lethal.

The package contains Pop Rocks® candy,
which explodes harmlessly when eaten.

Case 14

THE CASE

Two weeks after a heavy rain, Nancy walks into the forest with her trusty pooch. Together, they investigate numerous pine and fir trees. In a small pit dug by a rodent, Nancy finally finds the hidden treasure she's after.

THE MYSTERY

What is Nancy looking for and who might want it?

CLUES

The item can cost up to $1,000 dollars per pound.

Most often, the item is black in color.

In some European countries, people who collect this item are tested and licensed by the state.

The hidden treasure is edible.

Pigs and dogs are used to sniff the item out.

Nancy is looking for truffles, a delicacy prized by gourmands and chefs around the world.

30 SECOND
MYSTERIES

WHAT

Case 15

THE CASE

Jack works with leather and focuses on developing new ways to support people. Jack's work often causes women great pain. While Jack's victims don't know Jack, they sometimes pay large sums of money to experience the results of his professional efforts.

THE MYSTERY

What ís Jack's occupation and how does it support people?

THE CLUES

Some of Jack's biggest clients are really in step with fashion.

Jack's creations always have numbers stamped on them.

Jack purposely looks toward the ground when he's walking down the street.

Jack works in leathers, though he doesn't have to wear leather to work.

Jack is a designer, but he doesn't make jeans.

Jack is a shoe designer. His shoes support people by protecting their feet.

30 SECOND MYSTERIES

WHAT

Case 16

THE CASE

A man prepares for a dangerous mission at work by putting on a constricting uniform. Halfway through the mission, he senses danger and immediately presses a button. He escapes that threat, but moments later is found 100 feet away unconscious. He later dies.

THE MYSTERY

What is the man's occupation and what was the cause of death?

THE CLUES

The man was conducting scientific research.
The man's uniform came with special equipment.
When the man was found, he was soaking wet.
The man boarded a boat before embarking on his mission.
The man did not die from drowning.

The man was scuba diving. He inflated his vest, ascended too quickly and died of the bends (too much nitrogen in the blood).

30 SECOND MYSTERIES

WHAT

Case 17

THE CASE

A sweaty, out-of-breath individual walks into the offices of an upscale law firm. She saunters right past the reception area to the desk of a top partner. The partner hands her an envelope and then curtly dismisses her. Though she looks out of place here, her special services keep the partner very satisfied.

THE MYSTERY

What is this woman's job and where could she be found?

CLUES

The woman carries important, sometimes confidential, items.
The woman carries a radio so she can communicate with her office and her clients.
The woman is in excellent physical shape.
Strong leg muscles are a prerequisite for this woman's livelihood.
The woman's preferred mode of transportation has two wheels.

The woman is a bike messenger; she can be found cycling around any metropolitan area.

THE CASE

A group of four comes together and follows a road they believe will lead to enlightenment. The group's leader brings along a trusted companion. The group encounters alien animals, metaphysical phenomena and extreme allergies during its travels.

THE MYSTERY

What is the name of the leader's companion and in what city does the road end?

THE CLUES

All four members of the group sing.

You won't find the city on any map.

There are no signs on the road and it isn't paved.

The city is named after a precious gem and the road is made of brick.

The companion is a four-legged animal.

*The animal's name is Toto
and the road ends at the Emerald City.*

30 SECOND MYSTERIES

WHAT

Case 19

THE CASE

A man at work nervously handles a small metal device. He cautiously pours a flammable fluid into the device to create an intended reaction. It is important that he be very precise in his measuring. Most people see the resulting product as a good thing, but for some it may be life threatening.

THE MYSTERY

What is the man's job and what has he created?

THE CLUES

The product is often customized to the specifications of its buyer.

The product must be delivered in a specified container.

The product can have a debilitating effect.

The product cannot be purchased after 2:00 a.m. in California.

The product can be dry even when it is wet.

The man is a bartender and he made a martini.

Case 20

THE CASE

Jason feels perfectly fit. He has no symptoms of any disease and feels no pain. After a brief exam with a doctor, Jason is told that he needs surgery. After the operation, Jason starts bleeding profusely and is in excruciating pain. The doctor declares the operation a success.

THE MYSTERY

What kind of degree does the doctor have and what did the surgery accomplish?

THE CLUES

The doctor studied for many years to earn her degree.

Jason won't be bothered by this problem again.

The doctor is not a MD.

Jason lost four body parts during the surgery.

Surprisingly, Jason was just as smart after the operation.

CASE 20 SOLUTION

The doctor has a dental degree (DDS) and removed Jason's wisdom teeth.

Case 21

THE CASE

Sara must be extremely careful when entering and leaving her office building each day because it can be very dangerous. Once at work, she sits in the same spot and stares out of her office window. She does not change direction but change is a big part of her job.

THE MYSTERY

What is Sara's job and who are her clients?

CLUES

Sara works alone in her office.

The view from her window changes frequently.

At times she may be slow but others are constantly speeding around her.

She has a lot of money in her possession but does not spend it.

She often tells people where to go.

*Sara is a tollbooth collector and
her clients are drivers.*

30 SECOND MYSTERIES

WHAT

Case 22

THE CASE

Jay asks Brooke for her address to send her a letter. Brooke checks the mail everyday but the letter never comes. She later finds out that Jay was involved in a crash and could not get the letter to her. Jay is not injured and there is no damage to his car.

THE MYSTERY

What happened to Jay and whose fault was it?

CLUES

Brooke received all of her other mail.

Jay's Outlook is not a good one.

Jay called someone in the yellow pages to fix his problem.

Jay's work was affected by the crash.

Jay was not in his car when the crash took place.

Jay had Brooke's email address and his computer crashed. It was no one's fault.

THE CASE

Rob wakes up in the middle of the night after hearing a loud noise. He quickly puts on his shoes and runs outside where he finds several familiar faces. They all stand facing the building, but don't say a word. They fear disaster but are told to go back inside after a brief uneventful period.

THE MYSTERY

What sound did these people hear and what are they waiting for?

THE CLUES

They have all done this many times before throughout their lives.

Many were taught to do this in school.

All of them heard the same noise.

They are all neighbors.

The sound is meant to save the residents' lives.

Rob and his neighbors heard their apartment's fire alarm; they're waiting to be sure that it was only a false alarm.

Case 24

THE CASE

Sam has lived in the United States all of his life. He likes the military, but doesn't like wars. He works for the government, but isn't in politics. Everyone feels like they are related to him, but no one has actually ever met him.

THE MYSTERY

What is Sam's name and what is his government job?

THE CLUES

He is extraordinarily patriotic and is a spokesperson for military recruiting.

He began his work during World War I and has been working ever since.

He has white hair and a beard, and always wears a hat.

Sam is not a real person.

Sam's favorite colors are red, white and blue.

He is Uncle Sam, the image of patriotism, particularly during wartime.

THE CASE

Danielle coordinates the preparation of five, sometimes seven, highly elaborate meals a day. She never gets to eat any of these meals, even though she works so hard to get every ingredient just right. And what's more, Danielle will be the first to admit that she is actually not a very good cook.

THE MYSTERY

What is Danielle making and why doesn't anyone eat her meals?

THE CLUES

Danielle fell into this job by chance; she used to be an interior decorator.

Danielle works with a small army of assistants and collaborators to get her job done.

Danielle is not a chef.

She's always been more concerned about the look of a dish rather than its taste.

Danielle works with a photographer.

Danielle is a food stylist. She makes food look good so that it can be photographed.

Case 26

THE CASE

Michelle slowly slides her fingers against the silver blades in her hand to check their sharpness. Next, she glances in the mirror to see how she looks. Finally, she enters an area where a group of solemn people from around the world holds her in judgment. Michelle has not committed a crime nor has she entered a courtroom, yet the group's judgment may affect both her and her country.

THE MYSTERY

What is Michelle doing and why is she doing it?

THE CLUES

Michelle neither walks nor talks in front of the group.

Michelle realizes this could be her golden opportunity.

The climate is icy, yet Michelle wears very little.

Michelle takes her cues from the music.

Michelle is one of several women being judged.

*Michelle is a figure skater competing for
an Olympic gold medal.*

30 SECOND MYSTERIES

WHAT

Case 27

THE CASE

Thousands of people stand in the middle of a city street and look up into the sky at an enormous wild creature. The yellow creature hovers over the crowd and dives toward a group of schoolchildren standing near a famous department store. A group of men struggles to contain the creature with nets and ropes, hoping desperately to keep it from attacking the crowd.

THE MYSTERY

What is the creature's name and where can it be found?

THE CLUES

The creature is big and feathery.
There are other strange creatures flying in the same area.
The crowd has gathered for a national holiday.
The creature lives on a famous street.
Everyone thinks these creatures are full of hot air.

*The creature is Big Bird as a balloon float.
It can be found at Macy's Thanksgiving Day Parade
in New York City.*

THE CASE

Benjamin carries a book of matches in his pocket. Every night he walks into a room full of people, takes out the book of matches and mesmerizes each person in the crowd. He hears gasps, sighs and then applause, but he can't speak while the audience is reacting.

THE MYSTERY

What is Benjamin's profession and what does he do with those matches?

THE CLUES

It's likely that no one else in the crowd can do what Benjamin can.
Benjamin is an entertainer whose act calls for lots of suspenseful drum rolls.
He wears an elaborate costume when he works.
He is in a profession that has been around for thousands of years.
His act is hot stuff.

Benjamin is a fire-eater. He uses the matches to light the torches that he puts into his mouth.

WHERE

WHERE

Case 1

THE CASE

A 12-year-old girl walks into an establishment alone and picks up a magazine to read. She is then cornered, led to the backroom and instructed to sit still and be quiet. Fearing for her safety, she obeys this request, but is attacked with a sharp object anyway. By the end of the ordeal, she feels no pain and actually pays money to a woman before she leaves the place.

THE MYSTERY

Where is the girl and why does she pay the woman?

THE CLUES

The girl has avoided the building in the past.

The woman was expecting the girl.

The girl's mother was with her.

The woman has a lovely smile.

The girl was OK until she opened her mouth.

The girl is at the dentist.
She pays the woman for services rendered.

THE CASE

Nina finishes getting dressed and enters a crowded room. Even though Nina is neither a government agent nor a criminal, her every move is monitored by the roomful of people. Some are taking notes while others are actually photographing her. Nina doesn't smile and doesn't talk to a single person. She isn't frightened, but knows she'll be in trouble if she doesn't leave the room within about two minutes.

THE MYSTERY

Where is Nina and what is her occupation?

THE CLUES

Nina is not the only one in the room being watched.

Nina is getting paid for her participation.

Nina will enter the room again in 15 minutes.

It took Nina two hours to get dressed.

Nina is forced to change her clothes many times.

CASE 2 SOLUTION

Nina is on the catwalk at a fashion show.
She is a model.

30 SECOND
MYSTERIES

WHERE

Case 3

THE CASE

A small, defenseless animal stands quietly in the sunshine. Suddenly, it is hoisted up into the air by a rope and pummeled with sticks until its body is mutilated. Although many witness this, the perpetrators are not punished or condemned in any way.

THE MYSTERY

Where did this action take place and who did it?

THE CLUES

The action commemorated a festive occasion and anniversary.

The perpetrators could not see the animal as they hit it.

The animal is unusually colored.

The animal is light for its size.

The animal is only valuable for what can be found inside it.

The animal is a piñata pummeled by children at a birthday party.

THE CASE

After bidding goodbye to his daughter and granddaughter, an Englishman sets out from his small village on a long journey. Three years later he returns, only to find that his village is empty and has been abandoned for some time. Despite some clues and numerous searches, the fate of the village inhabitants is never discovered.

THE MYSTERY

Where is the village and what is it called?

THE CLUES

The man was English but he didn't live in England.
When the man left, the village had just been built.
The man could not return earlier due to war between England and Spain.
Sir Walter Raleigh visited the village.
The village is located on the coast of the Atlantic Ocean.

The village is the Lost Colony of Roanoke, located on Roanoke Island in North Carolina.

30 SECOND MYSTERIES

WHERE

Case 5

THE CASE

Chuck spends his time going door to door, performing unsavory tasks all day. He likes helping people and doesn't mind when he has to go to the hospital. Some people might treat him badly, but others are quite kind; whatever their disposition, they call on him when the going gets tough.

THE MYSTERY

How does Chuck earn his living and where can he be found?

THE CLUES

Chuck is in a helping profession.
He knows his clients inside and out.
Most of his clients wish they were in better shape.
Emergencies happen everyday in his workplace.
A stethoscope hangs around his neck.

Chuck works as a nurse at the local hospital.

THE CASE

Louis and Casey speak discreetly over the phone exactly one week after they robbed a bank together. They haven't seen each other since. Louis informs his partner that he has stashed the money, but refuses to divulge where it's hidden. Louis knows where Casey's kids live and makes Casey promise not to rat on him. Shortly after he hangs up, Louis is released from a locked room.

THE MYSTERY

Where is Casey and where is Louis?

THE CLUES

The call is not long-distance.

Casey isn't upset with Louis.

Louis is not a prison inmate.

Casey and Louis are partners in more than just crime.

While on the phone, the couple can see each other.

Casey is in prison and Louis (her husband) is visiting her.

THE CASE

A boy walks into a room alone and is taken to a seat by an older woman who is a stranger to the boy. He is strapped in and told he will not be able to communicate with his family for some time. He cries and begs to go, but is told to be quiet and sit still. Hours later the boy is freed and is told to leave the room. He doubts that he will ever see the older woman again.

THE MYSTERY

Where is the boy and who is the woman?

THE CLUES

The boy is not being punished.

The woman is just doing her job.

The boy's parents are waiting outside for him when he leaves the room.

The woman wears a uniform.

The boy leaves the room in a different city than when he entered the room.

The boy is on an airplane.
The woman is a flight attendant.

30 SECOND MYSTERIES

WHERE

Case 8

THE CASE

A woman immigrates to the United States from France. Although she lives in New York for many years, she never learns to speak English or hold down a job. Nonetheless, she becomes one of America's most famous residents.

THE MYSTERY

Where in New York does this woman live and who is she?

THE CLUES

The woman arrived in New York in June 1885.

The woman is unusually tall and statuesque.

The woman has a great view of the Big Apple from her home.

The woman is the only resident of the island she inhabits.

People come from thousands of miles away just to see the woman.

*The woman is the Statue of Liberty
and she lives on New York City's Liberty Island.*

THE CASE

George walks into a room and is handed a number. His belongings are taken from him and he is asked to take off his clothes. A uniformed man escorts him to a locked chamber. An hour later, he emerges from the chamber covered in dirt and sweat.

THE MYSTERY

Where is George and what is he doing?

THE CLUES

George's number was attached to a key.

Only a male was allowed to escort George to the chamber.

George goes through this ritual once a month.

George wore a robe after taking off his clothes.

George tipped the uniformed man $10.00.

George is at a spa having a mud bath.

THE CASE

Christopher, an American, traveled to a foreign country to visit John. John is the leader of this foreign state and is the first national leader that Christopher has ever met. Christopher leaves John after an hour and travels on to Italy to have pasta and a nap. While Christopher is traveling John decides to go to church and pray.

THE MYSTERY

Where did Christopher visit John and what is John's title?

THE CLUES

Christopher didn't have to roam too far.

Christopher must confess he has never been in this place before.

Thousands of visitors make the same journey every day.

Although neither John's grandfather nor father was named John, he is
   nonetheless the 2nd.

John is a religious leader.

CASE 10 SOLUTION

Christopher has taken a trip to the Vatican.
John is Pope John Paul II.

Case 11

THE CASE

Every morning Isabel leaves her apartment alone in the wee hours and goes to sit in a small room by herself. In the room she listens to music and talks out loud for four hours. No one else enters the room while she is there, but Isabel's sanity isn't questioned and she actually gets paid for this unusual behavior.

THE MYSTERY

Where does Isabel go every night and why is she there?

THE CLUES

The room is occupied 24 hours a day.
She is only one of many people who go into the room every day.
Isabel always stays in the room for exactly four hours.
Isabel isn't talking to herself.
The room is soundproof.

Isabel is a disc jockey and she uses the room to host her late-night radio show.

THE CASE

A woman and her boyfriend get all dressed up and go to a crowded place. They meet up with several of their friends and the man professes his love for her. The setting is peaceful and romantic, but then the boyfriend smashes something with his foot and everyone quickly leaves the premises.

THE MYSTERY

Where does the couple meet with their friends and why does the man smash something?

THE CLUES

After the violence, the two are no longer dating one another.

The boyfriend is not mad or unstable.

They take separate limousines to get there, but the woman and her boyfriend leave together in one.

The boyfriend destroys a glass as part of the event.

All of the observers drink champagne after leaving the premises.

*The couple is getting married in a synagogue;
in keeping with Jewish tradition, the new husband
breaks a glass at the end of the ceremony.*

THE CASE

The ground beneath a group of unsuspecting people gurgles and groans. Steam escapes from a hole nearby and suddenly a violent sound emanates. This is followed by a stupefying, white-hot display of force. Instead of running for their lives, the people step closer and gaze in wonder.

THE MYSTERY

Where are these people and what are they looking at?

CLUES

This phenomenon happens when water comes in contact with magma in areas of volcanic activity.

This display can be seen approximately every hour.

It can reach heights of 106 – 184 feet.

This natural attraction was named in 1870 for its consistent performance.

It can be seen in a national park.

They are in Yellowstone National Park,
looking at the Old Faithful geyser.

Case 14

THE CASE

Cristina is inspecting a cargo ship. She notices several problematic holes in the vessel's hull but doesn't make note of them or tell anyone about it. Although other inspectors surround her, none of them speak during the entire process.

THE MYSTERY

Where is the ship located and why don't the inspectors speak to each other?

THE CLUES

The inspectors know each other well and are not arguing.

They need special equipment to conduct this inspection.

Even though Cristina finds rooms filled with water, she's not alarmed.

Throughout the inspection, Cristina's feet don't touch the ground.

Cristina enters the ship without using a ramp or opening any doors.

Cristina and her colleagues are inspecting a ship that sunk to the ocean floor; their deep-sea diving equipment prevents them from talking.

Case 15

THE CASE

Monica watches a group of men standing around below her. She sees one of the men get caught trying to steal from the other, while another just stands there and does nothing. Suddenly, without warning, a crowd of people around her stands up, stretches their legs and begins to sing. Monica quickly joins in.

THE MYSTERY

Where is Monica and what does the crowd sing?

THE CLUES

Monica has been sitting in the same place for two hours.
Monica's husband is sitting next to her.
Monica's husband is wearing a silly-looking hat.
Monica ate a hot dog and a box of Cracker Jack® an hour earlier.
Monica is wearing sunglasses.

Monica is at a baseball game.
The crowd sings "Take Me Out to the Ball Game."

THE CASE

A woman stands before a group of people. She begins to flap her arms around wildly, moving her head in outrageous ways. She will do this for at least an hour, often longer. It's possible that she'll cry as she flails about.

THE MYSTERY

Where might this woman be found and what is she doing?

CLUES

The people in front of her are seated.
She studied for years to learn how to do this.
Her movements are actually instructions.
She holds a baton.
Everyone else holds an instrument.

She can be found in a concert hall,
conducting an orchestra.

THE CASE

A man watches as a dodgy-looking stranger gets into his car and speeds away. The stranger drives around the nearest corner and disappears before the man can say anything. After a momentary panic, the man decides to head to work and try to retrieve the vehicle later.

THE MYSTERY

Where was the man when his car was taken and when will he retrieve it?

THE CLUES

The man loves his car.

The man was running late to work.

The stranger drove the car into a concrete structure.

The man will have to pay money to get his car back, but it is not a bribe.

The man does the same thing five days a week.

The man is having his car parked in a garage;
he retrieves his car after work.

THE CASE

A retired man lives on an island in sunny California in the 1940s. He has a great view, which he stares at for many hours every day from his room. He gets free room and board and is surrounded by others of his kind. He lives out his final days on the island surrounded by very valuable real estate, but feels trapped and burdened nonetheless.

THE MYSTERY

Where does the man spend his final days and why does he feel trapped?

THE CLUES

A lighthouse stands on the island.

The island is now deserted.

The island is near a big city in a famous bay.

The man is no choirboy.

The man has committed a felony.

The man is on Alcatraz. He feels trapped because he's a prisoner with a life sentence!

WHERE

Case 19

THE CASE

In a large well-lit room, thirty people repeatedly attack a small group of scrawny kids. The people wield a large red object, applying as much force as possible. The victims are greatly upset and publicly humiliated by this beating, but they feel pressured into subjecting themselves to the same torment the very next day.

THE MYSTERY

Where is this taking place and why are the kids being hit?

THE CLUES

Almost every person in the U.S. has had a similar experience.

The group circles its victims.

A teacher is present, but does nothing to interfere.

If the object misses the kids, there is usually only a brief reprieve.

The children are laughing, but try hard to avoid the object.

Two teams of kids are playing dodgeball in the school gymnasium.

30 SECOND MYSTERIES

WHERE

Case 20

THE CASE

Vito leads a group of people into a dark room that's filled with an overwhelming odor. The people are silent the entire time they are in the room. If they speak too often or too loudly, Vito reprimands them.

THE MYSTERY

Where are the people and what is Vito's job?

CLUES

The people often laugh or cry.

All of the people are sitting down.

The odor is fresh and buttery!

The people have paid to be in the room.

The people will leave the room after about two hours.

The people are in a movie theater and
Vito is a theater usher.

THE CASE

Since the early 1960s a man has awoken each morning and put on his uniform to go to work. The man has a black beard and likes baseball. He loves island life and is the most recognizable resident of his country. He is known throughout the world.

THE MYSTERY

Where does the man live and what is his name?

CLUES

He is often seen in a green military cap.

He was briefly exiled from his country before returning to overthrow its government.

His country and the U.S. have had several conflicts since the 1960s.

He is the leader of his country.

The island is famous for its rum and cigars.

CASE 21 SOLUTION

The man is Fidel Castro and he is the leader of Cuba.

THE CASE

Melissa parks her car and enters a large building. She is stopped by a man in uniform and is asked to prove her identity or leave the building. Melissa is taken to a machine and several of her personal possessions are confiscated. She then eats a hotdog and waits patiently in a high security area until she can leave the premises and get on with her plans for the day.

THE MYSTERY

Where is Melissa and what is she waiting for?

THE CLUES

Melissa bought the hot dog in the building.

Melissa is concerned about a storm warning.

Melissa waits in the room for over an hour before she is permitted to leave.

The room Melissa sits in only has three walls.

One of the items confiscated is a pair of scissors.

Melissa is at an airport, waiting to catch a plane.

THE CASE

Two third-grade girls chat away on a street corner after school. A middle-aged man weighing about 250 pounds pulls his vehicle up to the corner and signals to the children. They have never seen him before, but they both get into the vehicle. He doesn't tell the children where he is taking them and slowly drives away.

THE MYSTERY

Where is the man taking the girls and what is his profession?

THE CLUES

The girls' teacher warned them about the man.
The man lures more than a dozen more children into his vehicle after the girls.
One girl thinks the man is creepy, but the others think he's nice.
The school hired the man.
The man has a special type of license.

CASE 23 SOLUTION

The man is the girl's new bus driver. He is taking them home from school.

THE CASE

A waterside bar and restaurant offers free beer at sunset during the summer. At the end of the summer, the owner reviews his records and realizes that not even one of his many customers took him up on his special offer.

THE MYSTERY

Where in the U.S. does this bar operate and why doesn't the owner ever have to give away any beer?

THE CLUES

The bar is located north of Chicago.
The bar offers this special every summer.
The bar patrons laughed when they read the beer special.
The bar owner was not surprised after viewing the records.
During the winter, it snows a lot.

The bar is in Alaska. The owner never has to give away any beer because the sun never sets there during the summer months.

30 SECOND
MYSTERIES

WHERE

Case 25

THE CASE

A woman is visiting a major city with her husband. As her vehicle crosses a landscaped area she hears a loud crack and then commotion ensues. Bullets fly and, while she isn't injured, the woman goes directly to the hospital. Her life is never the same, nor are the lives of millions of others who witnessed the incident.

THE MYSTERY

Where was the couple visiting and who was the woman's husband?

THE CLUES

The woman's husband worked for the U.S. government.

A former U.S. senator was in the car.

The couple was visiting the Lone Star State.

The year was 1963.

The shots fired resulted in a tragic death.

The woman's husband was President John F. Kennedy; the couple was visiting Dallas, Texas.

THE CASE

Over the years, explorers make their way through an area of unmatched scenic beauty. At first they experience awe, but then they see dollar signs. Exploitation leads to the expulsion of natives; eventually something has to be done or all will be lost. A tall man steps in and changes the course of history for this gorgeous place.

THE MYSTERY

Where is this natural wonder located and who was the man that helped save it?

CLUES

Giant sequoia trees are abundant here.

It can be found in a famous mountain range.

It became the first national park in the U.S.

Half Dome and El Capitan are two of this park's most famous sites.

The man who helped save it signed a bill in 1864 that made it an inalienable public trust.

The place is Yosemite National Park in California;
President Abraham Lincoln helped preserve it
for future generations.

THE CASE

A creature has been living in the same waters for decades. It has attacked several tourists and has frightened many locals. Although it always attacks at the exact same place, millions of people visit that very place year after year.

THE MYSTERY

Where is the creature always spotted and what kind of creature is it?

THE CLUES

The creature springs upon people with little warning.

People pay money to watch the creature attack.

The creature lives in Southern California.

There is a movie made about the creature.

The creature is actually just a machine, but it resembles a very big fish.

*The creature is spotted at Universal Studios;
it is a mechanical shark from* Jaws.

THE CASE

A group of desperate men takes refuge in a nearby church. The enemy approaches and the men are vastly outnumbered. A standoff ensues that lasts nearly two weeks. When the scuffle is over, all the men from inside the church are defeated and dead, but people think of them as heroes, not lunatics.

THE MYSTERY

Where in the United States can this church be found and what is its name?

CLUES

In Spanish, the name of this place means "cottonwood."

It's a well-preserved historic site.

It figured in the battle for one state's independence.

The enemy spoke Spanish.

It can be found in the Lone Star State.

It is the Alamo in San Antonio, Texas.

WHY

MYSTERIES

WHY

Case 1

THE CASE

Lucy is suffering from a dangerous and possibly fatal disease. Her family decides that she should undergo an operation, but Lucy is not told or consulted. The operation will be done by someone who has never operated on a human being before.

THE MYSTERY

Why isn't Lucy told and who operates on her?

THE CLUES

Lucy is a beloved member of her family.

Although Lucy graduated from school, she has no degree.

Lucy has a license, even though she can't drive.

Lucy's family makes all decisions for her.

The person who will operate on Lucy has a medical degree but is not a physician.

Lucy is a dog. A veterinary surgeon will operate on her.

THE CASE

Lulu leaves her house and goes into a nearby park. There she begins to eat a large amount of worms, chewing vigorously in order to break up their rubbery bodies. Strangely enough, she suffers no ill effects; in fact, she repeats her action a few days later.

THE MYSTERY

What kind of worms did Lulu eat and why didn't she get sick?

THE CLUES

Lulu is human.

Lulu did not get the worms in the park.

These worms are not found in the dirt.

Lulu's worms are native to Germany.

These worms come in a variety of flavors.

CASE 2 SOLUTION

*Lulu ate gummy worms. She didn't get sick
because they're an edible treat!*

THE CASE

Jill Svoboda is driven from her home in Los Angeles, CA to a government building. She meets an official who travels with her for a time and then directs her back to the building. At the building, Jill is fingerprinted and photographed, even though she has committed no crime. Jill drives home with a smile on her face.

THE MYSTERY

Why was Jill smiling and what agency does the official work for?

THE CLUES

The official works for the state.

This is the first time Jill has done this.

The official spends most of his time on the road.

No one speeds when they are with the official, but the official is not a police officer.

Jill spent months preparing for her visit to the building – and is only 16 years old.

The official works for the Department of Motor Vehicles; Jill is smiling because she just passed her driving test.

30 SECOND
MYSTERIES

WHY

Case 4

THE CASE

Several people learn that someone has been murdered. The people spend hours following the evidence and attempting to solve the crime. Finally, they identify and confront the suspected murderer, but they do not seek the murderer's arrest or even report the crime to the police.

THE MYSTERY

How do they identify the murderer and why don't the people report the crime?

THE CLUES

The murder occurs in a mansion.

The murder weapon is also discovered.

The people investigate by questioning one another.

The murder was committed with a revolver.

The murder took place in the conservatory.

The people are playing Clue®. They identify the murderer using the clues provided in the game.

Case 5

THE CASE

George attends a party, where he quickly gulps down a large iced tea before unexpectedly having to rush home. He suffers no ill effects but other people at the party who drink the iced tea become violently sick. Some even die.

THE MYSTERY

Why did the other people become ill and why didn't George?

THE CLUES

All the iced teas were exactly the same.

None of the iced-tea drinkers were allergic to any substances.

George has no special resistance to anything and drank his iced tea in under a minute.

Everyone drank an equal amount of iced tea.

The people were poisoned.

*The ice in the drinks was poisoned;
George drank his iced tea before the ice melted.*

THE CASE

Michael is fleeing a stampeding herd of buffalo when he comes to a wide, deep river. To escape, he must cross it, but there is no bridge and he has no boat or materials to make a boat. He cannot even swim. Nonetheless, he easily gets away.

THE MYSTERY

Why is Michael able to cross the river and why don't the buffalo follow?

THE CLUES

Michael has no special equipment.

The buffalo are excellent swimmers.

Michael is not particularly strong; in fact, he is small and slender.

Though the river is full, Michael does not get wet while crossing it.

The buffalo are large animals, weighing over 1,000 pounds each.

– · –

*Michael can cross the river because it is frozen;
the buffalo are too heavy to follow.*

THE CASE

A group of women attack an unarmed man, pummeling him mercilessly and attempting to inflict severe damage. When they finish, the man is not injured and the women gather around the man, waiting eagerly for him to speak.

THE MYSTERY

Why did the women attack the man and who is he?

THE CLUES

The women know the man and have attacked him before.
The women do not think that they will actually hurt him.
The man is paid to be attacked.
The man wears a special protective outfit.
The women are students.

---

*The women are in a self-defense class
and attack the man as part of their training.
The man is their instructor.*

Case 8

THE CASE

Marie and her best friend Rose are having a party. As the hostess, Marie entertains all the guests, but Rose just sits silently and stares at the wall. Marie serves her, but Rose never eats or drinks a thing. Soon Marie gets bored and puts Rose in a small room for the remainder of the evening. Luckily, Rose doesn't mind this at all.

THE MYSTERY

Why doesn't Rose mind the isolation and what type of party are they attending?

THE CLUES

The two friends are not fighting.
Rose acts this way all the time.
Food and drink are not required to make this party a success.
Rose is kept in a room with others like her, none of whom talk to each other.
Marie is in kindergarten.

They are at an imaginary tea party and Rose is a doll that is placed in a playroom.

THE CASE

A drunken man leaves his favorite bar at midnight and starts stumbling toward his home. By the light of a full moon, he decides to take a shortcut. Along the way, he trips, hits his head on a rock and passes out. He never regains consciousness and is dead by morning. Although his footprints are visible, his body is never found.

THE MYSTERY

Why is the man's body never found and how did he die?

THE CLUES

The man did not die of alcohol poisoning.

The fall did not kill the man, but it did knock him unconscious.

The man's body was moved from the spot where he fell, but not by people.

The man lived on the beach in Hawaii.

The man died just before high tide.

The man drowned and his body washed out to sea.

THE CASE

A woman is sitting at home in an easy chair reading a book when a masked man bursts in and snatches her purse. Although the man carries no weapon and is less than six feet from the woman, she makes no effort to stop him. She reports the crime to the police and provides a description of her purse, but gives no details about the masked man.

THE MYSTERY

Why didn't the woman describe the masked man and what is unusual about the book?

THE CLUES

The woman did not know the man, but she knew the man was breaking into her home.

The woman was reading *War and Peace,* by Leo Tolstoy.

The woman speaks only English.

The woman did not see the man.

The woman's hands were busy at the time of the break-in.

*The woman is blind and was reading
a book in Braille.*

THE CASE

Dr. Cooper, a registered surgeon, goes into surgery and immediately passes out. The operation is finished by the time that Dr. Cooper comes to. After a thorough physical, he is called upon to perform an operation on a young child. Even though the hospital authorities know that the patient will die if Dr. Cooper passes out again, no other surgeons are present.

THE MYSTERY

Why did Dr. Cooper pass out and why is he trusted to perform the operation on the child?

THE CLUES

Dr. Cooper is an experienced surgeon.

Dr. Cooper's operation was a success.

It did not surprise anyone that Dr. Cooper passed out.

Even after Dr. Cooper passed out, the operation could not have proceeded without him.

Dr. Cooper was not operating when he passed out.

Dr. Cooper passed out because he was given anesthesia; he can operate now that he is recovered from his surgery.

30 SECOND MYSTERIES

WHY

Case 12

THE CASE

Toni wanders methodically up and down the same few city blocks each day. She walks with purpose but takes her time. Every once in a while she stops, consults her surroundings and takes something out of her pocket. The folks who live in the neighborhood can't stand the sight of her.

THE MYSTERY

Why don't people like Toni and what is she doing?

CLUES

In her pocket is a pad of paper.

She's been berated more than once for doing her job.

Begging her doesn't help.

People run to their cars when they see her.

"Lovely Rita" is well known for doing this job.

Toni is a meter maid; she's disliked because she writes people parking tickets.

30 SECOND MYSTERIES

WHY

Case 13

THE CASE

Tami travels extensively and has visited seven countries in the past six months. Throughout her trip, she's stayed in luxurious five-star hotels and has taken advantage of every available amenity from room service to daily spa treatments. The management is well aware that she will skip out without paying but never confronts her about her clandestine freeloading. In fact, they invite her to come back again soon.

THE MYSTERY

Why is the hotel management so nice to Tami and what is her job?

THE CLUES

Tami always travels alone.

She does not work for any of the hotels in which she was staying.

None of the hotels in which she was staying are owned by the same company.

Tami does not accept bribes.

Tami takes thorough notes that will be published.

CASE 13 SOLUTION

The hotel management is nice to Tami because they want to impress her. She is a journalist who reviews hotels.

THE CASE

Alexandra spends her day making people wince, sometimes scream, in pain. But people seek her out and pay her money to do this work. Sometimes her clients may even bleed a little, but they almost always come back for more.

THE MYSTERY

What is Alexandra's job and why are her clients bleeding?

THE CLUES

Most of Alexandra's clients return to her month after month.

In many U.S. states, she cannot practice her craft without a license.

Alexandra likes to poke around at work.

The tools of her trade can all fit nicely in a small box, not much bigger than her hand.

People come to her with all kinds of ailments, from headaches to terminal illness.

*Alexandra is a licensed acupuncturist;
her patients sometimes bleed because they are
being stuck with needles.*

THE CASE

Josh loves mysticism, fun and adventure. Unfortunately, he wakes up one morning feeling heavy and notices his clothes no longer fit. Unable to figure out what's going on, he goes downstairs to greet his mother, who takes one look at him and screams. Dismayed, Josh immediately leaves home with no plans to return. After several weeks of trying to adjust to a new lifestyle, Josh returns home and everything becomes normal again.

THE MYSTERY

Why does Josh's mother scream and where does he go when he runs away?

THE CLUES

Josh's pajama bottoms seem to have shrunk and now go down only to his knees.
Josh doesn't recognize his own face when he looks in the mirror.
Josh vaguely remembers making a wish at a carnival the day before the incident.
Josh falls in love, but it can't last.
Josh runs away to a big bustling city.

The boy is Josh from the movie Big. *Josh's mother screams because he's turned into a 30-year-old man. He runs away to New York City.*

THE CASE

A man lives on the top floor of a high-rise apartment building. Every day he takes the elevator down and walks to work. When he returns from work, he often takes the elevator halfway up and then walks up the stairs the rest of the way to his apartment. However, on rainy days, he takes the elevator all the way up.

THE MYSTERY

Why does the man take the stairs part way up when it's not raining and the elevator all the way up when it is?

THE CLUES

The man doesn't like to ask for help.

The man does not prefer walking to riding the elevator.

The man carries an umbrella on rainy days.

The man was not a popular pick for basketball in gym class.

The man is shorter than his 11-year-old niece.

He is a midget (or little person) and he cannot reach the button for the top floor. On rainy days he uses his umbrella to press the button.

Case 17

THE CASE

A woman hugs her children tightly and kisses them goodbye. As she steps out the door, she falls and screams. The children watch in horror as she flails about for close to 20 minutes but do nothing to help her. Within an hour they are all one big happy family again and discuss the incident over a late lunch.

THE MYSTERY

Why did the woman fall and why did the children neglect to help her?

THE CLUES

The woman was alarmed by the incident but wasn't hurt by the fall.

The children couldn't have reached their mom, even if they wanted to.

The woman did not walk out of a house.

The children had a bird's eye view of it all.

The woman fell thousands of feet but had a soft landing.

CASE 17 SOLUTION

The woman jumped out of an airplane. The children didn't help because she had a parachute.

THE CASE

Margaret devotes a long time to creating an abstract painting. She carefully considers where to place each brushstroke and which colors to use. Just as she is finishing her artwork, a woman approaches Margaret and sees the painting. The woman is immediately furious and puts Margaret in solitary confinement.

THE MYSTERY

Why is Margaret in solitary confinement and who is the woman who put her there?

THE CLUES

The subject matter of Margaret's painting is not at all offensive.
The woman has been pleased with Margaret's paintings before.
Margaret picked an unusual location for her artwork but was not breaking the law.
The woman has punished Margaret with this solitary confinement before.
Margaret is five years old and knows the woman well.

The woman is Margaret's mother; Margaret was punished because she drew on the wall.

30 SECOND
MYSTERIES

WHY

Case 19

THE CASE

Two sworn enemies take to the seas during wartime, employing their respective naval fleets for battle. With cunning strategy and precise battle plans, each hopes to outwit the other. Even though it's all-out war, each side is sure that none of its recruits will perish during the fighting.

THE MYSTERY

Why aren't the enemies worried about casualties and what is this battle called?

CLUES

Gunners await the command on both sides.

Fire will be exchanged one shell at a time.

Neither fleet is on the ocean.

The battle will not be over until one fleet is sunk entirely.

It will take between two and three hits to sink each vessel.

The enemies aren't worried about fatalities in this "war" because they're playing the game Battleship®.

THE CASE

At an ancient boarding school, a small girl awakes in the middle of the night in great pain. She's rushed to the hospital for an emergency operation. Her mother and father don't make it to the hospital but she doesn't seem to mind. She's comforted by her school friends. Millions of others know her by name.

THE MYSTERY

Why is the little girl so well known and what is her name?

CLUES

When she and her classmates go out, they walk in two straight lines.
She lives in Paris.
The house where she stays is covered with vines.
She loves winter, snow and ice.
She is the title character in books and movies.

The little girl is Madeline, the star and namesake of the series of children's books by Ludwig Bemelmans.

Case 21

THE CASE

A lonely man falls in love with a beautiful foreign woman. The woman is a great swimmer but is afraid to go in the water. The man loves the water, but prefers the woman.

THE MYSTERY

Why is this woman afraid of water and who is she?

THE CLUES

The man gives the woman a new name.

The woman saved the man's life once, a long time ago.

The woman is tall, blonde and beautiful, but sometimes her skin is scaly.

The woman learns the man's language by watching TV.

The man and woman are characters in a movie based on an old fairy tale.

*The woman is Madison from
the movie* Splash. *She is afraid because she
turns into a mermaid in water.*

Case 22

THE CASE

Jim and his family leave their home in San Francisco and drive seven hours, where they find themselves in a world built by foreigners. Although the creators of this world are known for their impressive building materials, this site does not look fit for human habitation. Jim is tired after the long drive but feels compelled to stay and examine the area for hours.

THE MYSTERY

Why does Jim feel compelled to stay for so long and what is the foreign world called?

THE CLUES

The family drove south.

The family stopped at McDonald's in Carlsbad, California and ordered two Happy Meals®.

The family has toyed around with the idea of visiting this world before.

Jim is carrying lots of cash.

Jim's kids love construction toys.

The foreign world is Legoland®.
The family stays because they are on vacation.

THE CASE

Ed Motch closes his eyes and ingests a large amount of a potentially fatal substance. This substance can cause nausea, vomiting, restlessness and seizures. Ed does not need a prescription from a doctor and the substance is not marked as toxic. However, in large enough doses it may result in death. Despite this, Ed ingests some of this substance every day at the same time.

THE MYSTERY

Why doesn't the substance kill Ed and when does he ingest it?

THE CLUES

The substance has no medical benefits for Ed.
If Ed doesn't ingest the substance, he may get headaches.
The substance is popular in Italy, Austria and the United States.
Sometimes the substance is powdered; sometimes it's liquid.
The substance is usually black or brown.

The substance does not kill Ed because it is just a cup of coffee. He drinks it first thing in the morning.

THE CASE

A large creature lives in Brazil. It has no claws, fangs or venom, but is the most dangerous creature in the world. Other animals flee at its approach and, where it goes, death and destruction sometimes follow.

THE MYSTERY

Why is the creature so dangerous and what is this creature called?

THE CLUES

The creature is adaptable and can live in a wide variety of climates.

The creature can run, swim, climb and even fly, but is the best at none of these.

Although the creature is dangerous, it is often terrified of small animals.

The creature excels over all other species in only one way.

Although the creature lives in Brazil, its relatives are found throughout the world.

The creature is a human being.
It is dangerous because it sometimes does not use
its intelligence well.

Case 25

THE CASE

Fred is allergic to most animals and avoids them whenever possible. Nonetheless, he owns a small mouse, with which he spends hours every day. He often holds or strokes his mouse, even though he doesn't love it.

THE MYSTERY

Why isn't Fred allergic to his mouse and where does he keep it?

THE CLUES

Fred has owned several mice in the past.

Fred does not keep his mouse in a cage.

If Fred lost his mouse, he would get another right away.

Fred's mouse does not move unless he pushes it.

Fred's mouse does not eat or drink.

Fred isn't allergic to his mouse because it's a computer mouse. He keeps it next to his computer.

30 SECOND MYSTERIES

WHY

Case 26

THE CASE

At night in a quiet neighborhood mobs of people move through the streets, using threats to extort handouts from the residents. Although they continue their behavior for several hours, no one reports them to the authorities or even complains.

THE MYSTERY

Why are these people moving through the streets and what threat do they make?

THE CLUES

Many of the people are frightening to look at.

The residents knew this would happen ahead of time.

The people are not doing anything illegal.

The handouts are edible.

This is an annual event that takes place every fall.

The people are children in Halloween costumes who want candy when they say "Trick or treat!"

30 SECOND MYSTERIES

WHY

Case 27

THE CASE

George, who owns a chemical factory, decided to murder his wife. To hide his crime, he attempted to destroy her body by dissolving it in a vat of concentrated acid. His wife's body and clothing completely disintegrated, but the authorities were nonetheless able to find evidence of her presence in the vat.

THE MYSTERY

Why didn't George's plan work and what evidence did authorities find?

THE CLUES

Although George owns a chemical factory, he doesn't know much about chemistry.

The evidence could be seen by anyone.

No one but George's wife could have left the evidence.

The evidence was small but heavy.

It's ironic that it was a gift from George that revealed his crime.

The authorities found the wife's gold wedding ring at the bottom of the vat. George's plan failed because gold only dissolves in aqua regia (a mixture of sulfuric and nitric acids).

30 SECOND
MYSTERIES

WHY

Case 28

THE CASE

In a small Scottish town, a tiny bundle of joy arrived a few years ago. Although she looked ordinary in every way, she was anything but. Scientists and curiosity-seekers alike took great interest in her birth, and soon people the world over knew her by name.

THE MYSTERY

Why was this birth so important and what kind of creature was born?

THE CLUES

She has no father.

She shattered many myths.

Her existence presents ethical dilemmas.

The way she was created may not work for every animal.

She is an identical copy of an adult mammal.

It was Dolly the sheep, the first cloned mammal.

Always ahead of the game, Bob Moog's newest undertaking is truly novel. As a game inventor, his credits include such favorites as 20 Questions® and 30 Second Mysteries®. As the CEO of University Games, he has propelled the company he founded with his college pal into an international operation that now boasts five divisions and over 350 products. Whether hosting his radio show "Games People Play," advising MBA candidates or inventing games, Bob sees work as serious fun. He now brings his flair for fun and learning to the bookshelf with the Spinner Books line.

Enjoy Spinner Books?
Get an original game!

Find these games and more at AreYouGame.com
or your nearest toy store.

2030 Harrison Street, San Francisco, CA 94110
1-800-347-4818, www.ugames.com